THE GREAT BIBLE

DISCOVERY

SOLOMON

THE BIBLE IS A BEST-SELLER. IT IS ALSO ONE OF THE MASTER-WORKS OF WORLD LITERATURE - SO IMPORTANT THAT UNIVERSITIES TODAY TEACH 'NON-RELIGIOUS' BIBLE COURSES TO HELP STUDENTS WHO CHOOSE TO STUDY WESTERN LITERATURE.

THE BIBLE POSSESSES AN AMAZING POWER TO FASCINATE YOUNG AND OLD ALIKE.

ONE REASON FOR THIS UNIVERSAL APPEAL IS THAT IT DEALS WITH BASIC HUMAN LONGINGS, EMOTIONS, RELATIONSHIPS. 'ALL THE WORLD IS HERE.' ANOTHER REASON IS THAT SO MUCH OF THE BIBLE CONSISTS OF STORIES. THEY ARE FULL OF MEANING BUT EASY TO REMEMBER.

HERE ARE THOSE STORIES, PRESENTED SIMPLY AND WITH A MINIMUM OF EXPLANATION. WE HAVE LEFT THE TEXT TO SPEAK FOR ITSELF. GIFTED ARTISTS USE THE ACTION-STRIP TECHNIQUE TO BRING THE BIBLE'S DEEP MESSAGE TO READERS OF ALL AGES. THEIR DRAWINGS ARE BASED ON INFORMATION FROM ARCHAEOLOGICAL DISCOVERIES COVERING FIFTEEN CENTURIES.

AN ANCIENT BOOK - PRESENTED FOR THE PEOPLE OF THE SECOND MILLENNIUM. A RELIGIOUS BOOK - PRESENTED FREE FROM THE INTERPRETATION OF ANY PARTICULAR CHURCH. A UNIVERSAL BOOK - PRESENTED IN A FORM THAT ALL MAY ENJOY.

M publishing
CARLISLE, UK

9

Later generations remembered Solomon for his wealth, for the Temple he built, and for his wisdom. But also for his marriages with pagan princesses. And because he was the last king who ruled over all twelve tribes.

Solomon was rich because of the victories his father had won. The kingdom he inherited had been united under David and its frontiers had been extended. Ruling over a large, prosperous kingdom, Solomon was able to raise taxes in various ways and to engage in international trade.

He also spent a great deal of money. His people felt the burden of meeting the costs of his splendid court and of his many building projects. Many of the men were conscripted as forced labour.

One of the building projects was the Temple, which was right next to Solomon's palace. A magnificent building, it stood for three centuries - until the Babylonians destroyed it.

Solomon was remembered for his wisdom. This will have included not only the kinds of saying we find in the Book of Proverbs but also knowledge of the natural world - what we might call botany, zoology, geology. Unfortunately his wisdom doesn't seem to have included leadership skills. People didn't feel as warmly towards this great king as they had towards David, the shepherd who became a warrior and then a king.

Nor did Solomon's wisdom always include 'the fear of the Lord', which the Bible says is "the beginning of wisdom". The prophets of the Lord will have been especially concerned by the fact that he allowed his foreign wives to worship their gods in Jerusalem. Perhaps it is not surprising that, after what had seemed such a splendid reign, Solomon's kingdom fell apart after his death. Appearances are often deceptive.

1 Kings
Proverbs
Song of Songs

SOLOMON

First published as *Découvrir la Bible* 1983

First edition © Librairie Larousse 1983

24-volume series adaptation by Mike Jacklin © Knowledge Unlimited 1994
This edition © OM Publishing 1995

01 00 99 98 97 96 95   7 6 5 4 3 2 1

OM Publishing is an imprint of Send the Light Ltd.,
P.O. Box 300, Carlisle, Cumbria CA3 0QS, U.K.

Introductions: Peter Cousins

British Library Cataloguing in Publication Data
A catalogue record for this book is available from the British Library
ISBN 1-85078-213-x

Printed in Singapore by Tien Wah Press (Pte) Ltd.

KING DAVID WAS VERY OLD. HE CALLED ONE OF HIS SONS AND THE PROPHET NATHAN TO HIS BEDSIDE.

COME HERE, MY SON

SOLOMON, SERVE YOUR FATHER'S GOD WITH ALL YOUR HEART, AND IN EVERYTHING OBEY HIS WILL...

SOLOMON
THE MAN OF PEACE

...BECAUSE IT IS YOU WHO'LL BE KING AFTER ME ON THE THRONE OF ISRAEL AND JUDAH.

SCENARIO: Etienne DAHLER
DRAWING: Carlo MARCELLO

3

A FEW WEEKS LATER...

THEY SHOULD TAKE DAVID DOWN TO JERICHO. HE WOULD BE MUCH BETTER THERE.

IT'S TOO LATE. THE KING ISN'T WELL ENOUGH TO TRAVEL ANY MORE.

...Y BROUGHT A YOUNG GIRL NAMED ...SHAG TO SERVE DAVID AND CARE ...HIM.

MEANWHILE ADONIJAH, ONE OF DAVID'S SONS, WAS PLOTTING TO SEIZE THE THRONE...

IS EVERYBODY HERE?

JOAB HAS COME. WE'RE STILL WAITING FOR ABIATHAR THE PRIEST.

PRINCE, SON OF DAVID, EVERYBODY HERE IS ON YOUR SIDE.

DAVID IS MUCH WORSE. TODAY I WANT TO KNOW WHOM I CAN COUNT ON.

...ONLY A SMALL PART OF THE ARMY, ADONIJAH.

...AND WHAT ABOUT THE PRIESTS, JOAB?

ABIATHAR!

I'M ALONE. ZADOK REFUSES TO FOLLOW YOU, AND AS FOR NATHAN THE PROPHET, DON'T EVEN TALK ABOUT HIM!

THAT IS NOT MUCH, JOAB!

IF YOU CAN'T BECOME KING BY FORCE, DO IT BY A TRICK!

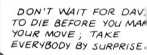

DON'T WAIT FOR DAVID TO DIE BEFORE YOU MAKE YOUR MOVE; TAKE EVERYBODY BY SURPRISE.

AB ADVISED ONIJAH TO MAKE RE THAT HIS OTHERS WERE ON SIDE.

DON'T WORRY! DAVID WON'T HAVE THE STRENGTH TO HIT BACK...

...AND WE WON'T HEAR ANY MORE TALK OF YOUNG SOLOMON!

LIVE KING!

ADONIJAH IS KING!

LONG LIVE THE KING OF ISRAEL!

BATHSHEBA, I'VE JUST HEARD THE PEOPLE ARE CALLING ADONIJAH KING, AND DAVID KNOWS NOTHING ABOUT IT! YOUR SON SOLOMON IS IN GREAT DANGER!

NATHAN TOLD BATHSHEBA WHAT SHE OUGHT TO DO TO SAVE HER SON...

YOUR MAJESTY, YOU PROMISED ME THAT SOLOMON WOULD BE KING AFTER YOU, AND NOW THE PEOPLE ARE CALLING ADONIJAH KING!

ADONIJAH! WHAT RIGHT HAS HE GOT TO ACT LIKE THAT?

BRING ZADOK, NATHAN, AND BENAIAH HERE!

TAKE SOLOMON TO GIHON AND ANOINT HIM KING OF ISRAEL. THEN SEAT HIM ON MY THRONE.

AND I'LL GIVE ORDERS THAT HE IS TO BE KING ISRAEL AND JUDAH!

DAVID'S ORDERS WERE CARRIED OUT AT ONCE...

IN THE NAME OF THE LORD, AND BY ORDER OF DAVID, YOU'RE KING OF ISRAEL!

LONG LIVE SOLOMON!

SOLOMON IS OUR KING!

PRAISE THE LORD!

NATHAN, HOW MARVELLOUS!

YES, SOLOMON, IT'S SPRING AGAIN, AND YOU ARE KING.

SOME WEEKS LATER...

DAVID!

I WANTED TO SEE JERUSALEM ONE LAST TIME...

IT'S BEAUTIFUL, AND YOU'LL MAKE IT A JEWEL...

A FEW DAYS LATER DAVID DIED. HE HAD REIGNED IN JERUSALEM 33 YEARS.

I'M TAKING THE ROAD EVERYBODY HAS TO WALK... SOLOMON, BE A MAN!

WHEN I WALK IN THE VALLEY OF THE SHADOW OF DEATH, I WILL NOT BE AFRAID, BECAUSE YOU ARE WITH ME, LORD. YOUR ROD AND YOUR STAFF PROTECT ME.

SOON AFTER SOLOMON HAD BECOME KING, BATHSHEBA CAME TO THE PALACE.

MOTHER, I'M SO HAPPY TO SEE YOU!

I'VE COME TO ASK YOU A FAVOUR.

ADONIJAH WANTS TO MARRY ABISHAG, THE YOUNG GIRL WHO SERVED DAVID UNTIL HE DIED.

BUT THEN HE WOULD BE CLAIMING TO BE THE KING!

HE IS YOUR ELDEST BROTHER... HE SHOULD BY RIGHT HAVE BEEN KING.

HE HASN'T CHANGED! I MUST PUNISH THIS CRIME OF HIGH TREASON...

HAT S THE ING AY?

THAT YOU HAVE TO DIE, ADONIJAH!

SOLOMON SENT BENAIAH TO HIS BROTHER.

FOLLOWING HIS FATHER'S ADVICE, SOLOMON RID HIMSELF OF HIS ENEMIES.

ABIATHAR! I WON'T TOUCH YOUR LIFE, BECAUSE YOU CARRIED THE COVENANT BOX IN FRONT OF MY FATHER.

GO TO YOUR FARM IN ANATHOTH. I NEVER WANT TO SEE YOU AGAIN!

AS FOR JOAB, HE TOOK FRIGHT, AND FLED TO THE TENT OF GOD.

NO ONE WILL DARE TO TOUCH ME HERE!

HE WON'T COME OUT. HE SHOUTED, 'I'LL DIE HERE!'

WELL, BENAIAH, DO WHAT HE SAYS!

THAT WAS HOW ABNER'S MURDERER DIED.

BENAIAH, I APPOINT YOU COMMANDER OF MY ARMY.

ZADOK, FROM NOW ON YOU ARE THE HIGH PRIEST OF THE LORD.

SO SOLOMON GAINED CONTROL OVER THE KINGDOM.

...KNOW, UNCLE ...UEL, I OFTEN GO ...GYPT, AND SOLOMON ...FEARED AND ...ECTED THERE, TOO.

...AH, THIS IS ISRAEL'S GOLDEN AGE! ...OU'VE SEEN NOTHING YET...

YOUR MAJESTY, THE KINGDOM HAS NEVER BEEN SO STRONG, BUT POWER BREEDS JEALOUSY...

WHAT SHOULD I DO?

MAKE SURE THAT THERE WILL BE PEACE BY MAKING MANY ALLIANCES.

BEGINNING WITH...?

EGYPT! THE PHARAOH HAS A DAUGHTER...

AN AMBASSADOR ASKED IF SOLOMON COULD MARRY HER...

I AGREE. THE PRINCESS CAN TRAVEL WITH YOU AND MY SERVANT WILL GO WITH HER...

HERE IS THE PRINCESS!

IN SOLOMON'S PALACE...

AFTER THE WEDDING THERE WERE GREAT CELEBRATIONS.

GOOD LUCK!

GOD BLESS YOU!

SOLOMON OFFERED A SACRIFICE AT GIBEON, THE MOST FAMOUS ALTAR.

LORD, ACCEPT THIS AS A THANK-OFFERING, AND LEAD ME BY YOUR WORD...

...OMON SPENT THE NIGHT ...THE ALTAR... AND, ...JACOB, HE HAD ...A DREAM.

LORD, GIVE ME THE WISDOM I NEED TO RULE YOUR PEOPLE, AND TO KNOW THE DIFFERENCE BETWEEN GOOD AND EVIL.

I WILL DO WHAT YOU HAVE ...SKED. I WILL GIVE YOU MORE ...ISDOM AND UNDERSTANDING THAN ...NYONE HAS EVER HAD OR EVER WILL HAVE AGAIN.

I WILL ALSO GIVE YOU WHAT YOU DID NOT ASK FOR: WEALTH AND HONOUR.

...K IN JERUSALEM SOLOMON OFFERED SACRIFICES ...ONT OF THE COVENANT BOX, AND GAVE ...ST FOR ALL HIS OFFICIALS.

17

IN A STREET IN JERUSALEM...

TELL ME MORE ABOUT SOLOMON...

HE'S A VERY CLEVER RULER. BECAUSE THE TRIBES COULD BREAK THE UNITY OF THE KINGDOM, HE DIVIDED IT INTO TWELVE DISTRICTS.

THE TWELVE DISTRICTS OF SOLOM KINGDOM. EACH ONE WAS SUPERVI BY A GOVERNOR, AND HAD TO SUP THE FOOD FOR THE KING AND HIS HOUSEHOLD FOR ONE MONTH OF THE YEAR.

JUDAH (separate arrangements)

SOLOMON MUST BE VERY RICH...

YOU CAN SAY THAT AGAIN SOME PEOPLE SAY THAT EVERY YEAR HE GETS MOR THAN 600 TALENTS OF GOLD!*

EACH DAY THEY HAVE TO SUPPLY 30 COWS AND 100 SHEEP, NOT TO SPEAK OF THE POULTRY. FORTUNATELY WE OF THE TRIBE OF JUDAH ARE NOT INCLUDED IN THAT PLAN.

* About 21 tonnes

BUT WHERE DOES IT ALL COME FROM?

THERE ARE TAXES EACH PRINCE HE RULES OVER HAS TO PAY EVERY YEAR...

EVEN PEACE CAN BE BOUGHT!

HE CONTROLS THE MAIN ROUTES LINKING MESOPOTAMIA AND EGYPT...

THE TRADE ALONG M.!

THOSE CHARIOTS WERE BOUGHT IN EGYPT; THEY'LL BE SOLD IN SYRIA.

AND THE HORSES?

THEY COME FROM CILICIA. SOLOMON WILL KEEP THE BEST FOR HIMSELF, AND THE OTHERS WILL BE SOLD TO EGYPT!

TELL KING SOLOMON THAT HE CAN HAVE ALL THE WOOD HE WANTS. FOR HIS PART, HE CAN SUPPLY FOOD FOR MY MEN.

I NEED WORKMEN! MAKE MEN COME FROM ALL THE TOWNS THAT WE'VE CONQUERED AND ALSO FROM ISRAEL!

THEY BEGAN TO CUT DOWN THE PRECIOUS TREES...

WE HAVE TO CHOP DOWN THESE CEDARS, BUT HOW WILL THEY BE TAKEN TO JERUSALEM?

FROM JERUSALEM TO TYRE, NEARLY 200 KILOMETRES.

TYRE

Phoenicia

MEGIDDO

BETHSHAN

JOPPA

SHECHEM

Jordan

BETHEL

JERUSALEM

FROM TOWN AFTER TOWN THE MEN WHO HAD BEEN CALLED UP JOINED THE GROUPS OF WORKERS...

GET A MOVE ON! YOU HAVE TO BE AT BETHSHAN TONIGHT!

ABOUT 30 000 MEN WERE SENT TO LEBANON, 10 000 A MONTH. THEY WORKED FOR ONE MONTH, THEN SPENT TWO MONTHS BACK HOME.

THE CEDAR TRUNKS WERE TAKEN DOWN TO THE SEA.

IN THE WATER THEY WERE TIED INTO RAFTS...

...THEN TOWED ALONG THE COAST AS FAR AS JOPPA. FROM THERE THEY WERE HAULED TO JERUSALEM

LOOK THERE! SOLOMON DOESN'T DO THINGS BY HALVES!

HE'S RIGHT! NOTHING IS TOO GOOD FOR GOD!

I'VE FINISHED MY MONTH OF WORK! I'M OFF HOME!

A GREAT WOOD DEPOT WAS SET UP ALONG THE WAY, WITH 3300 FOREMEN IN CHARGE.

HE STONES QUARRIED IN ISRAEL ERE SHAPED BY WORKMEN FROM YRE AND GEBAL.

HIRAM'S WORKMEN WERE EXPERTS AND GAVE VALUABLE HELP.

DON'T PUSH YOUR LUCK! THE PHOENICIANS ARE FUSSY!

THIS IS THE PLAN OF WHAT YOU HAD IN MIND.

THE TEMPLE OF SOLOMON

MAGNIFICENT!

INSIDE IT IS EVEN MORE BEAUTIFUL, YOUR MAJESTY.

SEVEN YEARS AFTER THE WORK BEGAN, THE HOUSE OF GOD WAS FINISHED.

NOW LET'S GO INTO THE INNER ROOM, THE HOLIEST PLACE OF ALL.

STAY HERE. I'LL GO INTO THE MOST HOLY PLACE ALONE.

SCENARIO: Etienne DAHLER
DRAWING: Carlo MARCELLO

HERE IS YOUR HOUSE, LORD MY GOD! MAY IT REFLECT YOUR GLORY.

EVERYTHING IS READY! NOW CALL TOGETHER ALL THE LEADERS OF ISRAEL, THE PRINCES OF THE TRIBES, AND THE CHIEFS OF THE CLANS, TO BRING THE COVENANT BOX TO ITS HOME.

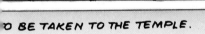

TO BE TAKEN TO THE TEMPLE.

THE GREAT DAY DAWNED, AND THE COVENANT BOX LEFT THE TENT...

SO MANY CATTLE AND SHEEP WERE SACRIFICED THAT THEY COULDN'T BE COUNTED.

THEN THE PRIESTS PLACED THE COVENANT BOX BETWEEN THE CHERUBS. THEY HAD TAKEN OUT THE POT OF MANNA AND AARON'S STAFF. ONLY THE TWO TABLETS OF THE LAW WERE LEFT INSIDE.

AS THE PEOPLE SANG HYMNS OF PRAISE, GOD'S GLORY FILLED THE HOUSE.

GIVE THANKS TO THE LORD, FOR HE IS GOOD...

...HIS LOV LASTS FOREVE

LORD, GOD OF ISRAEL, THERE IS NO GOD LIKE YOU IN HEAVEN ABOVE OR ON EARTH BELOW!

IN YOUR HOME IN HEAVEN HEAR THOSE WHO PRAY TO YOU IN THIS PLACE, AND BE MERCIFUL.

ALL THE ISRAELITES CELEBRATED FOR SEVEN DAYS.

ONE DAY SPENT IN YOUR TEMPLE IS BETTER THAN A THOUSAND ANYWHERE ELSE. I WOUL RATHER STAND AT THE GATE OF TI HOUSE OF MY GOD THAN LIVE IN TI HOMES OF THE WICKED.
Psalm 84

ON A VISIT TO A ZOO SOLOMON TOLD HIS ADVISERS EVERYTHING HE WANTED TO DO OUTSIDE OF JERUSALEM.

WE MUST FORTIFY EVERY TOWN AND VILLAGE...

THAT'S A GOOD WAY TO PROTECT THE PEOPLE AND EVERYTHING ELSE AGAINST THE ENEMY... PUT THEM IN A CAGE LIKE THESE BIRDS!

EXACTLY! I WANT THERE TO BE PEACE, AND THAT IS HOW I'M GOING TO MAKE SURE OF IT.

THOSE WHO LIVE IN PEACE ARE HAPPY PEOPLE ... THAT IS WELL WORTH SOME SACRIFICES.

ALL OVER THE KINGDOM PEOPLE WERE BUSY BUILDING.

THE IMPORTANT TOWNS WERE GIVEN GARRISONS.

DAN, CHECK NUMBER 431'S HORSESHOES!

WE CONTROL TRADE ON THE LAND, BUT ON THE SEA WE HAVE TO DEPEND ON OTHERS!

MASTER, IT'S YOUR TURN NOW!

I WANT TO BUILD A FLEET!

BUT WHAT WILL KING HIRAM OF TYRE SAY ABOUT THAT?

CAN HAVE THE [MEDI]TERRANEAN SEA... [S]O I'LL ALSO INCLUDE [THE]M IN MY PLANS!

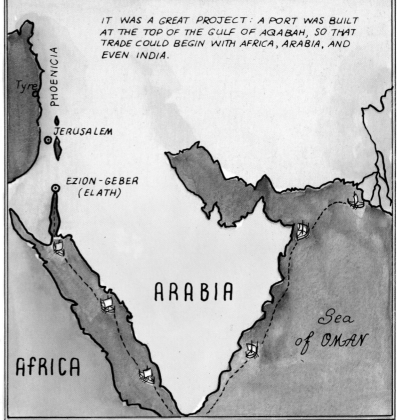

IT WAS A GREAT PROJECT: A PORT WAS BUILT AT THE TOP OF THE GULF OF AQABAH, SO THAT TRADE COULD BEGIN WITH AFRICA, ARABIA, AND EVEN INDIA.

PHOENICIA

Tyre

JERUSALEM

EZION-GEBER (ELATH)

ARABIA

Sea of OMAN

AFRICA

KING HIRAM AGREED TO SOLOMON'S PLANS, AND SENT WORKMEN TO HELP THE ISRAELITES BUILD THEIR FLEET.

AT LAST THE DAY ARRIVED FOR THE FIRST SHIPS TO SET SAIL FOR FAR-OFF LANDS, LOADED WITH CORN, WINE AND OIL.

THEY BROUGHT BACK ALL SORTS STRANGE THINGS... AS WELL AS 14 TONS OF GOLD.

WELL DONE! CONGRATULATIONS!

THERE'S EVEN BETTER TO COME: ONE OF OUR CREWS LANDED IN ARABIA AND MET THE QUEEN OF SHEBA.

SHE SENDS A MESSAGE TO TE YOU SHE'S COMIN TO JERUSALEM

SOON A STRANGE PROCESSION WAS SEEN TRAVELLING THROUGH THE KINGDOM.

SOLOMON'S PERSONAL GUARD ESCORTED THE IMPORTANT VISITOR ALL THE WAY TO JERUSALEM.

MAY THE LORD BLESS YOU, BECAUSE YOU HAVE COME TO THE VERY PLACE HE LIVES.

SHE GAVE HIM 4 TONS OF GOLD, SPICES AND PRECIOUS STONES. SOLOMON GAVE HER EVERYTHING SHE ASKED FOR. THEN SHE WENT BACK TO HER OWN COUNTRY.

SOLOMON OFTEN THOUGHT ABOUT HER AND THEIR TRADE AGREEMENTS... HE OFTEN FORGOT HER TOO!

SOLOMON BEGAN TO WORSHIP FOREIGN GODS, AND HE WAS NO LONGER COMPLETELY FAITHFUL TO THE LORD.

YOUR MAJESTY, LET ME WORSHIP THE GODDESS ASTARTE.

AND LET ME SERVE MILCOM, THE GOD OF MY FATHERS

DO WHAT YOU WANT. ANYTHING GIVES YOU PLEAS... MAKES ME HAPP...

SOLOMON IS BREAKING GOD'S LAW!

BUT WHO IS GOING TO TELL HIM SO? HIS PALACE IS FULL OF WOMEN. THERE IS NO LONGER ROOM FOR EVEN ONE PROPHET...

AS THE YEARS WENT BY, ... TOOK SO MANY WIVES THA... LOST COUNT OF THEIR NU... AMONG THEM THERE W... MANY FOREIGNERS, WHON... HAD FORBIDDEN THE ISRAELITES TO MARRY.

I DON'T LOVE THE LORD ANY LESS...

THE KING EVEN BUILT A TEMPLE TO FOREIGN GODS ON THE HILLSIDE OPPOSITE JERUSALEM.

THE SONG OF SONGS

THERE ARE MANY LOVELY SONGS IN THE BIBLE, BUT THE 'SONG OF SONGS', WHICH MANY THINK SOLOMON WROTE, IS THE BEST OF ALL.

A RABBI AND HIS DISCIPLES IN THE THIRD CENTURY BC.

SCENARIO: ETIENNE DAHLER
DRAWING: PIERRE FRISANO

RABBI, WHAT IS A SONG?

WHEN GOD MOVES SOMEONE'S HEART LIKE BREATH IN A REED FLUTE, THEN HE SINGS HIS SONG.

SOLOMON'S HEART WAS LIKE A YOUNG GIRL LOOKING FOR LOVE.

YOUR LIPS COVER ME WITH KISSES; YOUR LOVE IS BETTER THAN WINE.

BUT... WHO ARE YOU TALKING ABOUT?

ABOUT THE KING, THE GREAT KING...

HE WENT AS SUDDENLY AS HE C I DON'T KNOW IF I WAS DREAM BUT MY HEAR IS ON FIRE D AND NIGHT.

44